TURTLES

by Meg Gaertner

Cody Koala

An Imprint of Pop!
popbooksonline.com

abdobooks.com
Published by Pop!, a division of ABDO, PO Box 398166, Minneapolis, Minnesota 55439.

Printed in the United States of America, North Mankato, Minnesota.

092018
012019

THIS BOOK CONTAINS RECYCLED MATERIALS

Cover Photo: Shutterstock Images
Interior Photos: Shutterstock Images, 1, 5 (top), 5 (bottom left), 5 (bottom right), 6–7, 10, 12, 14–15, 17 (bottom left), 17 (bottom right), 18; iStockphoto, 9, 17 (top); Science Source, 21

Editor: Charly Haley
Series Designer: Laura Mitchell

Library of Congress Control Number: 2018950119

Publisher's Cataloging-in-Publication Data
Names: Gaertner, Meg, author.
Title: Turtles / by Meg Gaertner.
Description: Minneapolis, Minnesota : Pop!, 2019 | Series: Pond animals | Includes online resources and index.
Identifiers: ISBN 9781532162114 (lib. bdg.) | ISBN 9781641855822 (pbk) | ISBN 9781532163173 (ebook)
Subjects: LCSH: Turtles--Juvenile literature. | Fresh-water turtles--Juvenile literature. | Pond animals--Juvenile literature.
Classification: DDC 598.13--dc23

Hello! My name is

Cody Koala

Pop open this book and you'll find QR codes like this one, loaded with information, so you can learn even more!

Scan this code* and others like it while you read, or visit the website below to make this book pop.

popbooksonline.com/turtles

*Scanning QR codes requires a web-enabled smart device with a QR code reader app and a camera.

Table of Contents

Chapter 1

Pond Turtles

Turtles are **reptiles** with hard shells. They are found all over the world. There are more than 350 **species**.

Watch a video here!

Some turtles live in the ocean. But many turtle species live in freshwater ponds or lakes.

These pond turtles are found in North America, Europe, and Africa.

Chapter 2

Life in a Shell

Turtles have hard, smooth shells. The shell is the turtle's **ribcage**. It supports and protects the turtle's soft body.

Learn more here!

Most pond turtles have a shell that is brown or black on top. It has yellow spots or lines. The lower part of the shell is yellow and black.

Turtles cannot leave their shells. They pull their heads and feet into their shells to hide from danger.

Turtles look like tortoises, but they are different.

Tortoises stay on land. Turtles have **webbed** feet for swimming.

Chapter 3

In the Pond

Turtles swim a lot. But they also climb onto rocks or logs. Like other reptiles, turtles are **cold-blooded**.

Turtles sit in the sun to get warm.

Learn more here!

Turtles mostly spend time alone. They look for food during the day. Turtles eat plants and small animals.

Turtles make noise. They can sound like motors, burps, or barks.

Chapter 4

Growing Up

Turtles lay eggs on land. They dig a nest and bury the eggs. Then they walk away. Baby turtles are left on their own.

Complete an activity here!

Making Connections

Text-to-Self

Have you ever seen a turtle in real life? If not, have you seen another animal in the wild?

Text-to-Text

Have you read another book about a different animal? How is that animal similar to a turtle? How is it different?

Text-to-World

Turtles have shells to protect them. How do other animals protect themselves?

Glossary

cold-blooded – referring to animals whose body temperature varies with the temperature of the environment.

reptile – a type of animal that lays eggs and has scales, rough skin, or a shell.

ribcage – the set of bones that surrounds and protects an animal's insides.

species – a group of animals of the same kind that can have babies together.

webbed – connected by a thick piece of skin.

Index

Online Resources

popbooksonline.com

Thanks for reading this Cody Koala book!

Scan this code* and others like it in this book, or visit the website below to make this book pop!

popbooksonline.com/turtles

*Scanning QR codes requires a web-enabled smart device with a QR code reader app and a camera.